Too Cute!

Baby Squirrels

by Elizabeth Neuenfeldt

BELLWETHER MEDIA
MINNEAPOLIS, MN

Blastoff! Beginners are developed by literacy experts and educators to meet the needs of early readers. These engaging informational texts support young children as they begin reading about their world. Through simple language and high frequency words paired with crisp, colorful photos, Blastoff! Beginners launch young readers into the universe of independent reading.

Blastoff! Universe

Reading Level — Grade K

Grades 1-3

Grade 4

Sight Words in This Book 🔍

are	in	play	them
at	like	run	they
do	look	see	to
eat	many	soon	up
get	more	the	use
have	not	their	

This edition first published in 2023 by Bellwether Media, Inc.

No part of this publication may be reproduced in whole or in part without written permission of the publisher. For information regarding permission, write to Bellwether Media, Inc., Attention: Permissions Department, 6012 Blue Circle Drive, Minnetonka, MN 55343.

Library of Congress Cataloging-in-Publication Data

Names: Neuenfeldt, Elizabeth, author.
Title: Baby squirrels / by Elizabeth Neuenfeldt.
Description: Minneapolis, MN : Bellwether Media, 2023. | Series: Blastoff! beginners: Too cute! | Includes bibliographical references and index. |Audience: Ages 4-7 | Audience: Grades K-1
Identifiers: LCCN 2022012973 (print) | LCCN 2022012974 (ebook) | ISBN 9781644876732 (library binding) | ISBN 9781648347191 (ebook)
Subjects: LCSH: Squirrels--Infancy--Juvenile literature.
Classification: LCC QL737.R68 N48 2023 (print) | LCC QL737.R68 (ebook) | DDC 599.36--dc23/eng/20220322
LC record available at https://lccn.loc.gov/2022012973
LC ebook record available at https://lccn.loc.gov/2022012974

Table of Contents

A Baby Squirrel!

Look at the
baby squirrel.
Hello, kit!

Kits live
in **nests**.
The nests
are in trees.

nest

Most kits have many **siblings**.

siblings

Life as a Kit

Newborn kits
do not have fur.
They cannot see.

newborn
kits

Kits drink
their mom's milk.
Older kits
eat nuts.

Kits get bigger.
They grow
more fur.
Their tails
get fluffy!

Kits learn
to climb.
They use
sharp **claws**.

claws

Kits like to play.
See them run!

All Grown Up!

Kits soon
leave home.
Kits grow up fast!

Baby Squirrel Facts

Squirrel Life Stages

newborn   kit   adult

A Day in the Life

eat nuts   climb   play

Glossary

claws

sharp nails

nests

homes for squirrels

newborn

just born

siblings

brothers and sisters

To Learn More

ON THE WEB

FACTSURFER

Factsurfer.com gives you a safe, fun way to find more information.

1. Go to www.factsurfer.com.

2. Enter "baby squirrels" into the search box and click 🔍.

3. Select your book cover to see a list of related content.

Index

The images in this book are reproduced through the courtesy of: Eric Isselee, front cover, p. 4; Robert Eastman, pp. 3, 22 (newborn, kit); Rosa Jay, p. 5; Gay Bumgarner/ Alamy, pp. 6-7; Georgi Baird, pp. 8-9; Sumio Harada/ SuperStock, p. 10; Joe Blossom/ Alamy, pp. 10-11; Remi71, p. 12; BLFootage, pp. 12-13; Beth Baisch/ Dreamstime, pp. 14-15; Miroslave Hlavko, p. 16; Jay Ondreicka, pp. 16-17, 22 (eat); Juhku, pp. 18-19; Coffeemill, pp. 20-21; IrinaK, p. 22 (adult); Jan Philipp Kreysing, p. 22 (climb); A.Sergienko, p. 22 (play); W. de Vries, p. 23 (claws); Maximillian cabinet, p. 23 (nest); R - kirankumar, p. 23 (newborn); avsmal, p. 23 (siblings).